I Can Touch

Julie Murray

Abdo
SENSES
Kids

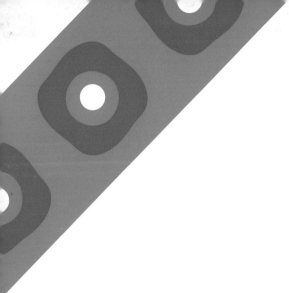

abdopublishing.com

Published by Abdo Kids, a division of ABDO, PO Box 398166, Minneapolis, Minnesota 55439.
Copyright © 2016 by Abdo Consulting Group, Inc. International copyrights reserved in all countries.
No part of this book may be reproduced in any form without written permission from the publisher.

Printed in the United States of America, North Mankato, Minnesota.

052015

092015

 THIS BOOK CONTAINS RECYCLED MATERIALS

Photo Credits: iStock, Shutterstock

Production Contributors: Teddy Borth, Jennie Forsberg, Grace Hansen

Design Contributors: Candice Keimig, Dorothy Toth

Library of Congress Control Number: 2014958415

Cataloging-in-Publication Data

Murray, Julie.

 I can touch / Julie Murray.

  p. cm. -- (Senses)

ISBN 978-1-62970-929-1

Includes index.

1. Touch--Juvenile literature.   I. Title.

612.8'8--dc23

              2014958415

Table of Contents

I Can Touch

There are five senses.

Touch is one of the senses.

We touch with our hands.

We touch things all around us!

We touch soft things.

Lisa sleeps with her **blanket**.

We touch **smooth** things.

Eric's blocks are smooth.

We touch cold things.

Abby makes a snowball.

We touch wet things.

Ted feels the water.

We touch furry things.

Ava pets her cat.

It can hurt to touch some
things. Be careful!

What did you touch today?

21

The Five Senses

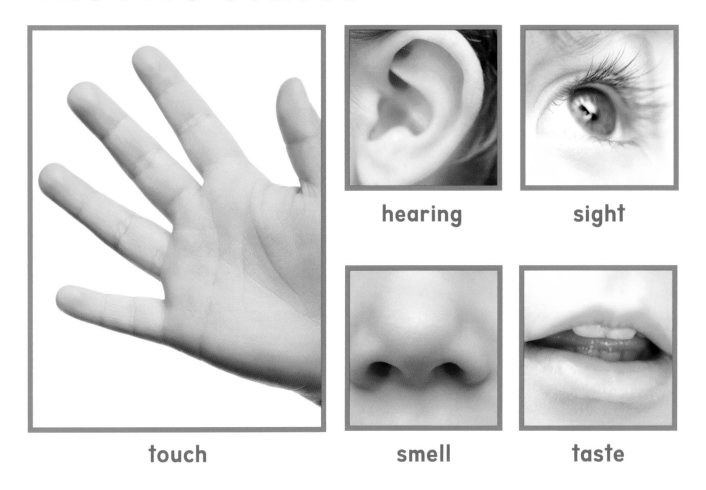

touch

hearing

sight

smell

taste

Glossary

blanket
a large piece of material used for warmth.

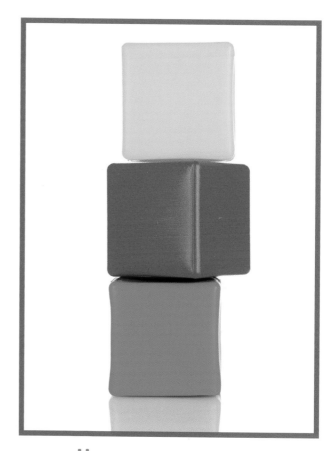

smooth
having a flat surface with no bumps.

Index

abdokids.com

Use this code to log on to abdokids.com and access crafts, games, videos, and more!

Abdo Kids Code:
SIK9291